Winston Churchill

The incredible life, legacy, and lessons from Winston Churchill!

Table of Contents

Introduction

Thank you for taking the time to pick up this book: Winston Churchill.

This book talks about the story of Winston Churchill, and shares some of his greatest lessons about life.

You will soon discover the greatest triumphs and failures of Winston Churchill, including those from his time at war, political battles, and long and tumultuous time in the public eye.

There are many lessons to be learned from Winston Churchill, a man with incredible persistence and achievements in a range of fields.

At the completion of this book, you will have a good understanding of Churchill's incredible journey, and will be able to use his experiences to enhance your own life!

Once again, thanks for choosing this book, I hope you find it to be interesting!

Chapter 1:
Family Life

History has quite a long list of great leaders who have done many great things in honor of their countries. But none of these leaders bear the distinction of being the first to stand up against a tyrannical power that has brought misery to millions of people. Winston Churchill did just that when he stood up against Nazi Germany in the Second World War. But before delving deeper into his war-time adventures, it's best to read up on his early experiences first to better understand the man that he became later on.

Winston Churchill belonged to Britain's nobility. He was born into a family that can trace its roots to as far back as the medieval period. Winston Leonard Spencer-Churchill was born on the 30th of November, 1874 at his family's palatial home, Blenheim Palace in Oxfordshire. His mother was Jeanette Jerome, a rich American socialite from New York. His father, Lord Randolph Churchill, was one of the leading figures in the Tory (Conservative) party at the House of Commons.

Winston spent his early years (aged 2-6 years old) in Dublin where Lord Randolph was serving as his grandfather's private secretary. It was in Dublin where Winston was first exposed to education through the efforts of his governess, Elizabeth Ann Everest. Because of his parents' constant absence, the young Winston formed a close relationship with Everest. She served not only as his nanny but also as his educator and confidante. Moreover, Everest became a substitute mother for the young Winston.

Nevertheless, Winton's parents were still present enough in his life to properly note his progress in school. They sent him to three different independent schools. At the first two schools, Winston gained a reputation for being an independent-minded boy. He also got into a few scrapes, which prompted his parents to get him transferred to Harrow. He didn't stand out academically in any of the schools that he attended. Despite their frequent absence from their son's early life, both parents still maintained regular correspondence with the young Winston throughout his academic years.

It is clear that Winston adored his mother dearly. But he also got to a point in his adolescence when he complained about her seeming neglect of him. Lady Randolph Churchill was often preoccupied with her social engagements and was known to take long travels abroad without either of her sons.

Winston had only one brother, John Strange Spencer-Churchill, also known as Jack. According to some historical reports, the two boys were close while growing up. However, many historians are baffled at why Winston tried to erase any traces of his brother in his memoir *My Early Life*. There are some passages in that book wherein he simply refers to Jack as 'that boy' or 'the boy' while recounting their boyhood adventures together. Unlike Winston, Jack was more academically-inclined and frequently earned better grades.

Jack contributed a lot in keeping their family afloat during the crash of Wall Street after WWI and the ensuing Great Depression. While Winston was working on their father's biography, Jack is credited with doing most of the research work. Jack was also highly supportive of Winston's career until his death in 1947. Historians argue that neglecting to mention his brother in any way was by no means done with any malice on Winston's part. He simply took his brother's presence as such a normal part of his life that he became quite thoughtless of it in the long run.

Historians also believe that between Lord Randolph and his wife, the father was the one who cared more for their two sons. His absence in their lives came as a result of his active role in British politics. But he also kept tabs on his sons mostly through correspondence, though he also often expressed disappointment in Winston's lacklustre academic performance. He was instrumental in paving the way for their military careers, though Jack's career was short-lived. In 1883, he set up his will to ensure that his sons would continue to live well after his death.

Unfortunately, their mother took advantage of the fortune that Lord Randolph left for his sons to fund her own social ambitions. The effect of this was felt more by Jack than by Winston. It was also Jack who discovered her misdeed 14 years later. Despite her seemingly selfish ways, or maybe because of it, Jennie supported Winston's political ascent. She did this to the point wherein she used her substantial social influence many times for the benefit of his career.

Winston Churchill's military genius can be explained by the fact that he descends from two families with military backgrounds. His ancestor on his father's side was Lord John Churchill, the first Duke of Marlborough. Lord John is considered by historians as one of the greatest generals in England. Throughout his military career, Lord John won numerous campaigns against the French. He is credited for being the one to neutralize the French King Louis XIV, also known as France's 'sun king'.

On Winston's mother's side, he is descended from a family whose ancestors fought during the War of Independence. His maternal grandfather, Leonard Jerome was married to Clara Hall. Both of them had grandfathers who either fought alongside General George Washington at Valley Forge or who fought in other notable battles in New York and Connecticut. There is also a popular notion that Clara Hall-Jerome had Native American blood. She is said to be descended from the brave Iroquois nation.

Chapter 2:
Academic Life

Winston Churchill's first school was the St. George's Preparatory School at Ascot, which was a boarding school for young aristocratic boys. Winston was only 7 years old when he first arrived at St. James. The young boy found it quite difficult to live life away from his family. The school did not provide him with enough space to study the subjects that he was truly interested in, such as History, Geography, and English. To top it off, the school also employed harsh means of discipline on its students.

These disciplinary methods included flogging the boys with the use of a birch stick. Understandably, the young Winston was also quite lonely at the boarding school. This loneliness caused him to exhibit a rebellious behavior that only grew worse as his homesickness deepened. All this contributed to the deterioration of his health, which then led the family doctor to prescribe his removal from St. George's post haste. He was then sent to Brighton, a small seaside school where he spent three relatively peaceful years.

Despite the relative comfort of the Brighton boarding school, Winston was still a very lonely young boy. He often wrote to his mother to come see him at school. His behavior also hadn't improved much. His teachers reported that he was a bright student though he was slovenly and quite negligent of his studies. Teachers also often complained about his constant tardiness.

At the age of twelve, Winston was enrolled at Harrow. He entered the school at the bottom of the class due to the low score that he got on the entrance examination. His low standing became another source of disappointment for Lord Randolph. In later years, it has been revealed that even Winston himself felt dissatisfied by his academic record prior to military school. However, he did have one source of pride in those days: his phenomenal memory. This skill won him a prize at Harrow after he recited 1,200 lines from a poem titled *Lays of Ancient Rome*.

Despite his low academic standing, Winston had fun during his years in Harrow. Being at the bottom of the class also gave him the chance to study English at length. This served as a good foundation for the journalistic career that he eventually chose in adulthood. His low academic ranking did not mean that Winston was a slow learner, though. His teachers often reported to his father that his intelligence ought to have placed him at the top of the class. But just like in Brighton, he was also careless and quite often tardy in Harrow and this affected his class standing.

However, he did excel in the subjects that he was really interested in. An example of this was when their class was given the task of drawing a map of any country. Winston chose to draw a map of New Zealand and was able to execute it excellently because of his interest in Geography. After graduating from Harrow in April of 1893, Winston then proceeded to study at Sandhurst. He failed to gain entry into Sandhurst twice before finally getting admitted on his third try.

He attended the Royal Military Academy for a total of 16 months, after which he started his active military service.

One notable factor that probably also contributed to Churchill's low standing in school was his speech impediment. No one can be certain about what the impediment was exactly.

Some historians say that he stuttered, while some believe it was merely a lisp that caused him to constantly mispronounce the s's. One thing that's sure is that it was often a cause for aggravation on the great man's part. But this impediment didn't stop him from living his dream of being a great orator.

He followed his doctor's advice and constantly practiced until he could say his speeches perfectly. In later years, he was aided in this pursuit by his wife, the Lady Clementine Churchill nee Hozier. He was also given a set of dentures that were specially designed to aid him in his speeches.

Chapter 3:
Military Career and Journalistic Career

Winston's entrance to Sandhurst would have been a reason for his father to finally be proud of him. However, it proved to be another source of disappointment and a point of contention between father and son. Lord Randolph wanted his son to join the 60th Rifles (the infantry) but Winston's low grades on the entrance exam only qualified him for the cavalry. Despite his father's disapproval, Winston chose to remain in the cavalry mostly because it did not require him to learn a subject that he always hated: math.

Joining the cavalry was a source of happiness for the 18-year-old Churchill. While there, he grew to love riding a horse. This is a hobby that he maintained throughout his adult life. His time at Sandhurst was also the best time in his entire academic life. He was able to make use of his skill in drawing maps thanks to his deep interest in Geography. He also felt that he and his classmates all started on an equal footing wherein no one knew more than what everyone else knew.

This positive change was apparent through the fact that for the first time since Winston entered formal school, he was finally going to graduate at the top of the class. His high class ranking qualified Churchill for a spot in the infantry but he did not grab that chance. He remained with the cavalry though he now bore the rank of second lieutenant in the 4th Hussars. Through these developments, Winston Churchill finally gained his father's approval.

But Lord Randolph had the chance to bask in the glow of his newfound pride for his eldest son for only a month. He died on the 25th of January 1895. Barely a month later, on the 20th of

February, Winston received his first commission and embarked on a military journey that would take him uphill, downhill and everywhere in-between. During the early years of his military career, Churchill worked more as a war correspondent than as an army officer. He was sent to battlefronts in Cuba in 1895 to observe the ongoing war between Cuba and Spain. He was commissioned by the Daily Graphic to write about that war.

Churchill's mother started to play a more active role in his life once he started his military career. It was with her extensive help through her connections that he was able to obtain commissions to various battlefronts. She was also responsible for his developing the habit of reading in his free time. This habit eventually became useful in his journalistic career. After Cuba, he was sent to the following places:

1. British India - He first stayed in Bombay and was then transferred to Bangalore. It was during this time that Churchill first started to extend his knowledge through self-education. He learned all that he could on subjects like economics, history, and politics. Through his mother's urgings, he read books like Gibbon's *The Rise and Fall of the Roman Empire* and Plato's *Republic*. He also started forming his opinions and his knack for debate.

2. India's North-West Frontier - After failing to report on the Greco-Turkish War, which ended before he could even get there, Churchill turned next to the Second Anglo-Afghan War. It was here where he had his first real taste of war, fighting alongside General Jeffrey and the second brigade in Malakand. During the fighting, Churchill witnessed an officer being hacked to death by the enemy Pashtun tribe. He wrote about this

experience and titled it *The Story of the Malakand Field Force*, which reached publication in December of 1900. He also submitted his accounts of the siege to the *Daily Telegraph* and *The Pioneer*.

3. Egypt and Sudan - Churchill's next live battle happened in Sudan in September of 1898. It was the Battle of Omdurman, which he also wrote about in two-volume book titled *The River War*. One month after the battle, he was back on British soil.

Churchill resigned from the army in May of 1899. By this time, he had already received some level of acclaim for being a war correspondent. He had also published five books about his war-time exploits. But working as a war correspondent was done not only to augment the small income that he received from the army. As he told his mother in the beginning, it was also done to pave the way for his political career. This career started almost as soon as he got back home.

Chapter 4:
Churchill's Early Years in Politics

Churchill's entry into politics is consistent with his entry into every other institution since childhood: he failed in his first attempt. But, just like always, he never gave up.

This first attempt happened in July 1899 where ran as a candidate representing the seat of Oldham. His defeat in the election caused him to once again pull on his parent's connections so that he could be assigned to a high-profile war assignment. He was sent to South Africa to cover the Second Boer War for *The Morning Post*. While on the battlefront, he was captured and taken to the enemy's camp in Pretoria as a war prisoner. He managed to escape from captivity and wrote about it afterwards. This catapulted his fame and turned him into a minor hero in Britain.

He did not go home immediately. He rejoined the army and, along with his cousin, the Duke of Marlborough, subsequently led some troops to Pretoria to negotiate the freedom of its remaining prisoners. After that, he returned home to England and published some more of his written works. He also decided to run for another election to represent Oldham.

In 1900, a 26-year-old Churchill finally took his seat in the House of Commons as a member of the Conservative party. This was officially the beginning of his political career. The first thing he did was to go on a speaking tour around Britain and in some parts of the United States wherein he was able to raise £10,000. Although his dream of working alongside his father in parliament could no longer be realized, he still endeavored to continue Lord Randolph's legacy. Churchill was staunchly against Irish home rule, just as his father was.

As a member of the conservative Tory democracy, Churchill actively participated in debates. He voiced a strong opposition for the government's expenses in military campaigns. He also opposed the imposition of additional tariffs as proposed by Joseph Chamberlain, a Liberal Unionist who led the opposition in the House of Commons. Churchill's stands caused him to be deselected by his constituency in Oldham though he remained in the seat until the next election. He also had severe disagreements with several members of the Tory democracy.

These disagreements led him to literally cross the floor and transfer to the Liberal party after four years of serving with the Tories. The most compelling reason for this transfer was his advocacy for free trade. Another reason was the fact that he was still trying to emulate his late father's example. It should be noted that his biography work on Lord Randolph Churchill's life was written between 1903 and 1905.

Churchill was appointed as the Under-Secretary of State for the Colonies in 1905. It is on this post that he encountered yet another failure: he was cut short by the Conservative party while delivering his first speech as the Under-Secretary. The speech was in opposition to the policies presented by Lord Milner with regard to the handling of the countries that were defeated in the Boer War. But again, this failure did not hinder Winston Churchill from plodding on. He later successfully delivered a speech seeking Conservative support in the formation of the Boer Constitutions.

Other government positions that Winston Churchill held before World War I include:

- ➤ President of the Board of Trade, 1908. As President of the Board of Trade, Churchill achieved several relevant social reforms that are often referred to as the Liberal reforms. These include the following:

- The Miners Act of 1908 – this mandated 8-hour workdays for all mine workers.

- The Trades Boards Act of 1909 – this established the first-ever system of mandated minimum wages in Britain.

- The Labor Exchanges Act – this made it possible for the establishment of institutions that assisted unemployed people in finding work.

➤ Secretary of State for the Home Department, 1910. His primary achievement while holding this post was the passing of the National Insurance Act in 1911. The Act not only provided sickness benefits to the employed members of society, but also to the unemployed. He also played an indirect role in the passage of two controversial laws: the Parliament Act of 1911 and the People's Budget.

The People's Budget sought the equal distribution of wealth in Britain through the imposition of higher taxes on the rich. These taxes were then used to fund various programmes that focused on social welfare.

All of these social reforms became a reason for Churchill to be reviled by members of the autocracy. They saw it as a betrayal of the social class into which Winston Churchill was born. But this assumption is far from the truth since Churchill still held the view that a well-oiled society was one wherein the upper class continued to hold the reins of power while the working class were grateful followers.

Churchill was assigned to the office of the First Lord of the Admiralty in 1911. He held this post until World War I. Just as he did in parliament, Churchill also introduced important reforms in the navy. His first act was to replace all the Lord Commissioners of the Admiralty. He then formed a war staff that assisted him in introducing the reforms. These reforms include:

- Replacing the main armament of the navy's battleships with 15-inch guns.

- Developing the first Queen Elizabeth class battleships.

- Developing the Arethusa class 6-inch gunned cruisers.

Most importantly, Churchill switched the Royal Navy's power requirement from coal to oil. These reforms were shaped by the reforms that were famously introduced by the former Admiral of the Fleet, Lord John Arbuthnot Fisher. All of this was done in response to Germany's growing aggression.

Another important contribution that Churchill made while in the Navy prior to WWI was his staunch support for the Home Rule Act of 1914. In a nutshell, the Act gave Ireland the ability to govern itself and to have its own leaders, albeit still as a member of the United Kingdom. The united party of the Liberal Unionists and the Conservatives, also known as just the Unionists, were in strong opposition of the Act. In his usual style, Churchill gave speeches promoting the Act.

In doing so, Churchill once again earned the ire of his peers. However, it is interesting to note that this move is the first move he made that wasn't patterned after his father. In his lifetime, Lord Randolph was a leading figure in opposing the First Home Rule Bill that was introduced by Charles Stewart

Parnell in 1886. The succeeding incidents reflected a side of Winston Churchill that would be his most dominant characteristics throughout his career.

The primary characteristic that he displayed was the fact that he preferred to stand his ground when faced with an enemy. But once the enemy was vanquished, he was then ready to concede to their demands. As Churchill himself wrote on his autobiography, he would've wanted to defeat the Irishmen first and then give them Home Rule after their defeat.

Chapter 5:
World War I

Churchill was the leading figure that led Britain to victory against the Germans in World War II. This feat earned him a place in the ranks of some of the greatest men in history. But being a great strategist who won wars for Britain wasn't always his strongest suit, especially not during the First World War. When the war broke out in 1914, Churchill made the seemingly logical decision to seize 2 Turkish battleships that were being constructed in Britain. His order was carried out unceremoniously, which then prompted a then-neutral Turkey to form an alliance with Germany.

He also encountered a few more failures during the war, which eventually led to his demotion and subsequent resignation. His first failure happened in Antwerp, where he was stationed in 1914. Belgium had already proposed beforehand for Antwerp to be evacuated and then surrendered to the advancing Germans. But the British forces, which were made up of the combined Marine and Naval Brigades, remained firm. In the end, Antwerp still fell to the Germans after a prolonged siege.

Churchill was highly criticized for his role in Antwerp. He was questioned for what was deemed to be a waste of Britain's resources. There were also damaging rumors that Churchill was more focused on publicity instead of focusing on how to run his department effectively. His popularity in the Royal Navy had also taken a big hit after he replaced Sir George Callaghan and dismissed Prince Louis of Battenberg from his post as Admiral of the Fleet. The latter happened despite the fact that Louis' release was necessary due to his failing health and his growing unpopularity with the constituency because of German descent.

Churchill took all this in stride and instead focused on the development of the war tank. He sponsored its construction through providing financial assistance from the Royal Navy's research funds. He and then-Prime Minister David Lloyd George were of the same mind on this endeavor. The tanks were developed to improve Britain's capabilities in trench warfare. Churchill first got the idea for the tank when he witnessed an armoured tractor easily cut through a barbed wire fence during a demonstration. He proposed the use of the Holt tractor in developing sturdy tanks that did not have the same weaknesses as its predecessors.

Churchill next played a big role in the naval campaign in the Dardanelles Straits, which ended in another failure and thousands of casualties. From the beginning of the war, Churchill had always maintained his stand on the merits of an aggressive assault against the Ottoman Empire. He understood the importance of the Dardanelles because it provided accessibility to the Russian navy. Churchill's failure in capturing this important territory could be attributed to a lot of things. First off on the list was the fact that he was pressured to choose the most suitable replacement for First Sea Lord after Prince Loius' resignation.

Churchill ended up hiring the retired First Sea Lord John Fisher, who was already seventy years old by then. Their opinions and decisions were continually at odds throughout the whole campaign. Things came to a head when Fisher finally resigned from his post in May of 1915. The plan to force the Dardanelles into submission using naval attacks was put into action. Eventually, infantry were sent to supplement the naval forces. The order to attack was formally given by Churchill on the 3rd of November 1914.

The battle was initially in favor of the British, whose forces were augmented by ANZAC soldiers. However, both the natural and artificial fortifications of the Dardanelles eventually caused Britain's offensives to fail. The battle eventually progressed into the Gallipolli peninsula and came to be known as the Battle of Gallipoli. The battle lasted for 10 months and the results were disastrous not only for Churchill but also for the entire Allied forces. The deciding factor for their defeat was the fact that the Ottoman Turks had carefully observed their maneuvers for the past months. This enabled the Turks to strengthen their defences.

The defeat at Gallipolli cast a dark light on Churchill's legacy. It has been referred to more than once by a few historians as 'Churchill's folly'. However, other historians have argued that all of Churchill's decisions at that time were made in an attempt to prevent going to war with Turkey. The majority of the blame has always fallen on Churchill's shoulders since a lot of people have conveniently forgotten one important factor: Churchill was only in charge of the naval aspects of the battle.

Everything that happened on land were masterminded by the Secretary of War, Lord Horatio Herbert Kitchener and the Mediterranean Expeditionary Forces' Commander in Chief, General Ian Hamilton. There were many other people who played a part in formulating the strategies for the battle both on land and at sea. These people belonged to the highest levels of command, including Prime Minister Asquith. In fact, Asquith and Churchill often conferred with each other and they seemed to share the same views on various occasions. Churchill's resignation from the Admiralty was forced on him

by the Conservatives, with whom the Prime Minister had just
formed a new alliance.

Chapter 6:
Between the Two Great Wars

After the defeat in Gallipolli, Churchill bounced from one government job to another, though he maintained his seat in parliament. He was ready to accept any government position (in his own words: even the lowliest one) as long as he remained employed. He accepted the position of being a sinecure for the Chancellor of the Duchy of Lancaster. He eventually resigned from the post because he felt that his energy was unused. He also still bore a grudge against the undue amount of blame that he received for the Gallipolli fiasco.

Churchill's spirits were lifted once he was assigned to the fighting in France in January of 1916. He was given the temporary rank of Lieutenant Colonel and commanded the 6th Royal Scots Fusiliers battalion. The battalion had heard about Gallipolli, which meant that Churchill was not well-received into their ranks. But he soon won them over with a combination of personality, knowledge, and military experience. The men were also impressed by the fact that Churchill's leadership style was executed through turning himself into a good example for his men to follow.

He stayed with the battalion for six months, after which he decided to continue his battle in parliament. He rejoined parliament as a member of the opposition, whose leader by then was Sir Edward Carson. In a letter, Lloyd George called Churchill out for his decision to leave the army in the heat of battle just to make speeches in parliament. He says that this is a reflection of Churchill's tendency to put his needs first over that of his country.

Churchill was also assigned to other governrent positions, including:

> Minister of Munitions from July 1917 to January 1919 - His appointment required a lot of backroom negotiations between the new Prime Minister, David Lloyd George, and the few people who still supported Churchill. This proves just how unpopular he still was among his peers.

> Secretary of State for the War and Air Divisions from January 1919 to February 1921 - He was originally eyeing the post of Minister of Defence but his requests for appointment were continuously denied.

His first order of business in the War Office was to change the process by which soldiers were demobilized. The process that he inherited involved sending home the soldiers who were most needed in certain industries. This often meant sending home the men who had served in the army for the shortest period of time. The system had often caused unrest among the disgruntled soldiers. Churchill changed this system to make sure that the soldiers who had been serving for the longest time were the first to be released from military duty.

His greatest contribution as Secretary of State was the adaptation of the Ten Year Rule at the end of the First World War in 1919. The rule required the military to plan its expenditures with the assumption that it wouldn't engage in any major war in the next ten years. The goal of the rule was to give the British Treasury a better leverage at controlling the country's finances.

Churchill was also determined to re-establish himself in the political arena. In this light, he also made a lot of changes in the air force, such as:

- Reducing the size of the Royal Air Force to 4 Home squadrons and 18 Imperial squadrons.

- Rejecting the proposals for providing government support on civil aviation.

Churchill was also pre-occupied with the Russian Civil War. He strongly backed the idea of intervention in the war with the aim of crushing the Bolzheviks once and for all. To this end, he continuously worked behind the scenes to strengthen the British presence in various Russian territories. He sent secret and urgent memorandums to all the British commanders, tried to get the Allies to support his plans for intervention, and pushed for offensives in Northern Russia. He strongly supported the White forces in the Russian war and did what he could to send aid.

He was also instrumental in providing armed assistance to Poland in their invasion of Ukraine. Once again, his actions made him quite unpopular not only with his peers but with the Press as well. A bigger consequence of his actions during this time was the irreparable damage to his relationship with Lloyd George. His policy for responding to rebellion with armed offensives was also made clear when he sent the RAF to quell the rebellion in Somaliland. The same tactic was used for quelling another rebellion, this time in the British-held countries of Mesopotamia.

Churchill made the same stance during the Irish War of Independence. He responded to the IRA by establishing the Auxiliary Division and the Special Reserve Division (Black and

Tans) of the Royal Irish Constabulary. His stand changed when he became the Colonial Secretary in 1921. This time, he supported the idea of negotiations with the Irish Freedom Fighters. When the war ended, Churchill was one of the signatories on the Anglo-Irish treaty. The treaty effectively established the Irish Free State.

Churchill continued to work for the interests of Britain in his post as Colonial Secretary. He ensured that British presence in Egypt, which used to be part of the defeated Ottoman Empire, remained strong. This was done despite the constant uprisings by the Arab citizens of the country in a bid to dislodge the British from its stranglehold. British presence in Egypt was necessary to ensure that Britain's air routes to its other colonies remained open, especially the routes to India and the other oil-rich countries in the Middle East.

Churchill was also instrumental in putting the current ruling family of the Kingdom of Jordan in its current position. He created a Middle Eastern Department, which conferred in Cairo to discuss the fate of the states that once belonged to the Ottoman Empire. In this conference, two new Kingdoms were created: Iraq (now the Republic of Iraq) and Transjordan (now the Hashemite Kingdom of Jordan).

From 1922 to 1923, Churchill experienced several failures. First was when he lost during the elections in the Dundee constituency in October of 1922. He once again stood for the Liberal party in the general election of 1923, but this time in the constituency of Leicester. A few months later, he once again ran for election but this time he was no longer tied to any party. He referred to his candidacy as an Independent Anti-Socialist bid but lost with a narrow margin against his opponents.

During the general elections of 1924, Churchill was once again running as an independent candidate. But this time, he labeled himself as a "Constitutionalist". His candidacy was also backed by the Conservatives and this time, he won. In 1925, Churchill once again crossed the floor by rejoining his former colleagues in the Conservative party. Prior to his election as a member of parliament, Churchill had already been appointed as Chancellor of the Exchequer.

It was in this post that he once again bore the sole blame for a decision that took numerous discussions with several knowledgeable men to make: Britain's return to the pre-war currency, also known as the gold standard. This decision was announced in the budget for 1924. It had disastrous effects in Britain's economy, specifically in the coal mining industry. The effects were so bad that it eventually led to the 1926 General Strike of coal miners. Churchill himself later admitted that this decision was his greatest mistake.

Churchill became estranged from the Conservatives following the party's defeat in the general election of 1929. He had opposing views from the other members of the party in many issues, such as the issue of Indian Home Rule. He was bitterly opposed to this idea. The final straw came in 1931 when Churchill was ignored during the formation of Ramsay MacDonald's National Government.

This political isolation led Churchill to focus more on his writing. Some of the works that he finished during this period include:

> *Marlborough: His Life and Times*

> *A History of the English Speaking Peoples*

- ➤ *Parliamentary Government and the Economic Problem*

- ➤ *Great Contemporaries*

He also wrote a slew of articles and speeches. Writing became a primary source of income for him.

Churchill's opposition to Indian Home Rule was due to the fact that he believed Indian independence would cause widespread unemployment. The effects of this would be felt more by the United Kingdom and its citizens whose livelihood depend on the Indian economy than by India itself. Churchill also maintained that independence would cause widespread violence in India because the country was not yet prepared to bear the responsibilities of governing itself. The issue of Indian independence became such a great barrier between Churchill and then-Prime Minister Stanley Baldwin that it caused him to break from the coalition. Churchill never held any other government position again while Baldwin was Prime Minister.

Churchill's attitude towards bestowing independence to India is seen by some historians as a reflection of his deeply conservative views. He was seen as a pugnacious individual who was unable to accept major changes in society, especially the changes that brought the New Order to Europe during his time. But it is interesting to note that most of Churchill's predictions became reality in the years that followed the imposition of Indian Home Rule. This continued on to the years after WWII when India was working its way towards full independence from British rule.

Chapter 7:
World War II

Churchill had already been closely watching Adolf Hitler's movements since as early as 1930. He viewed Hitler as a potentially dangerous individual. He believed that Hitler was about to start another war in cohorts with his loyal followers. He expressed these sentiments while attending a dinner party at the German Embassy. Churchill shared these sentiments with the former Prime Minister, David Lloyd George.

In some of his writings, Churchill expresses a wish for Hitler to make use of his dictatorial nature to rebuild his country. But when Hitler and his Nazi posse rose the ranks to hold power in 1933, Churchill was the first to warn everyone of impending danger. In this light, he made several speeches to warn everyone, such as his speech on the 7th of February 1934. On that speech, Churchill advocated the rebuilding of the Royal Air Force, which had been significantly reduced during the budget cuts in the 1920's. In July of the same year, Churchill urged for the renewal of the League of Nations.

In 1936, Churchill was once again passed over in the appointment of a major government post. The post of Minister of Co-ordination of Defence was given to Sir Thomas Inskip, which surprised everyone including the appointee himself. This was surprising mostly because Churchill had been receiving some positive feedback from Chamberlain prior to the appointment. But Chamberlain did not assign him on that post primarily due to all the intrigue that surrounded his reputation.

Churchill's warnings about Hitler were ignored mostly because the populace was still weary from the effects of the First World

War. As a result, Britain stayed out of the Nazi's way and chose to ignore Churchill's sensible warnings. In 1938, the British government led by Prime Minister Neville Chamberlain agreed to give Germany a small portion of Czechozlovakia in exchange for Germany's promise of maintaining peace in the region.

Barely a year after the agreement was signed, Hitler reneged and staged an invasion of Poland. Churchill's predictions were once again coming true. Britain and its allies declared war against Germany in September of 1939. At this time, Churchill was re-instated as the First Lord of the Admiralty. The Phoney War happened and Churchill proposed that the allies occupy some towns in Norway and Sweden as pre-emptive moves against the Germans. This proposal was vetoed by Chamberlain and the other members of the War Cabinet.

Not long after that, the Germans invaded Norway and then followed this up with an invasion of France and the surrounding Low Countries. This resulted in the loss of confidence by the war cabinet on Neville Chamberlain and his subsequent resignation as Prime Minister. The search for his replacement was done quickly and he made some recommendations to King George VI as to who would be most-suited for the post. Eventually, Winston Churchill took over as the Prime Minister. The rest of the story, you can say, is history. There have been hundreds of books written about it. But what exactly was Churchill's contribution to the whole of humanity?

Note that from the beginning of his political career, Churchill had always been known for his speeches. This time, his knack for making noteworthy speeches became the glue that kept his country together during a dark and terrible time. His speeches electrified the members of parliament and quietened the politicians who wanted a negotiation with Hitler. It prepared the people for a lengthy period of being at war. It kept people's hopes up.

His war cry was to never surrender, not even when Britain seemed to be beaten from all sides or even when Britain stood alone after France fell. France was defeated in June of 1940 and it subsequently declared an armistice. In July of the same year, Britain was bombarded by air raids. These air raids were in preparation for the German ground forces that would invade soon after. Churchill refused to back down and ordered the Royal Air Force to meet the German bombers head on.

What followed was the Battle of Britain, which lasted for three months and was done entirely in the air. There were heavy losses on both sides. On land, Churchill was everywhere. He made speeches on the radio to let Britain's allies know that the country was not going to give up. He also rallied their support, of which most of them responded. The first countries to send back up forces were:

- Africa

- Australia

- Canada

- The Caribbean

- New Zealand

The US was initially reluctant to join the war. Churchill, with the invaluable help of his wife Clementine, set about to woo President Franklin D. Roosevelt into sending aid. Churchill was probably the only person who was glad when the bombing of Pearl Harbor happened. That's because it meant that America was now officially in the war. Russia joined in the fray soon after. This tilted the balance of power between the warring Allied and Axis powers. But the war was not won right away and the Allied forces, specifically Britain suffered more losses.

As Churchill had predicted in 1940, the war would last for 4 or 5 more years. The Allied powers had started to regain its footing after the US joined in. It was slowly regaining the territories that were seized by Germany in Europe and Japan in the Pacific. By July of 1945, Germany and Japan were forced into an unconditional surrender and Italy was subdued by Allied invasion. The war had officially ended and Winston Churchill was celebrated as the biggest hero of the day.

It was now time for Britain to face yet another challenge, something that Churchill had also predicted early on: the transition from war to peace. He foresaw that after Britain and its allies had claimed victory, problems were bound to arise due to the impending unemployment of the war veterans. Demobilization of the troops would also serve as another challenge, as well as the resumption of international trade. Churchill was all set to lead his country in facing these challenges after the war, but unfortunately, it wasn't meant to be.

Chapter 8:
Life after WWII

Churchill was deemed to be the best candidate for the job of being the Prime Minister while the country was at war. All the qualities that made him such a controversial figure in British politics before 1940 were the same qualities that bolstered his people's confidence from 1940-1945. He was a single-minded leader who stubbornly stood his ground in the face of a bigger foe. Unfortunately, once the war was over, these qualities could no longer be appreciated and Churchill's presence became redundant. The British people, wary of the seemingly endless wars, wanted someone whom they thought was more capable of leading them towards a peaceful existence.

As a result, Churchill and the Conservative party suffered a great loss in the 1945 general elections. Churchill was replaced as Prime Minister by Clement Attlee of the Labour Party, who also served as his deputy Prime Minister during the war. Churchill's neglect of the Conservative Party, to whom he belonged, during the war years also contributed to this defeat. Some of the leading members of the party have been heard to complain about this neglect. Despite this, Churchill remained as the party's leader until it won the general elections again 6 years later.

Churchill's status as a well-respected world leader kept him in the limelight even when he was no longer the prime minister. During the intervening years, Churchill actively supported and opposed the various proposals in parliament. He renewed his stand against giving India full independence. He believed that the current leaders were only serving their own interests and not the interests of the people. He also advocated for the creation of a union of European nations. This led to the formation of the Council of Europe in May of 1949.

Churchill also busied himself with making speeches at various institutions to promote the things that he believed should be a priority. One of his most memorable speeches during this time was when he dubbed the imaginary boundary that divided Europe into two as the Iron Curtain. This term stuck and has been used ever since in hundreds of history books. Churchill's predictions in the early years that Russia could develop into a threat also came true when Russia formed an alliance with Germany.

Russia continued to be a threat after the war despite the defeat of the Axis powers. Churchill did not hesitate in formulating a plan to end Russia's burgeoning threat during the Cold War. Records found in the FBI's archives show that Churchill tried to get US President Harry Truman to approve a pre-emptive nuclear strike on the Kremlin in 1947. If this was approved, Russia would have had no chance of launching a nuclear counter-offensive since they didn't develop their nuclear weapons until 1949.

When Churchill was not busy politicking, he kept his mind focused on writing. He finished writing his six-volume book that depicted his experiences and personal thoughts during WWII. The book is aptly titled *The Second World War*. The book is still sold in some of the leading bookstores in many countries including several online stores. It continues to receive great reviews from readers, which is a testament to Churchill's brilliant mind.

The book includes a sweeping view of what happened before, during, and after WWII, as well as a deeper insight on how Churchill's mind worked. In the book, Churchill relates how he felt destined to be elected as Prime Minister in 1940 and how everything he had been through since childhood had prepared him for what he called Britain's "darkest hour".

After 6 years of leading the opposition, Churchill was once again elected as Prime Minister in 1951. He was already 77 years old at the time, which is why it isn't surprising that he was no longer as sprightly as when he first held the post. In fact, Churchill often had to do his work in bed. Cabinet meetings also often turned into shouting matches as Churchill stubbornly refused to put on his hearing aids. His focus in this second term was to strengthen the relationship between the United States and Britain.

He had already made inroads during President Roosevelt's term and was trying to cement it in the succeeding terms of Presidents Truman and Eisenhower. Churchill was also hell-bent on maintaining the declining power of the British Empire. Churchill's brilliant strategic mind also foresaw another future scenario that the other people in power refused to accept: that of the opportunity for building a better relationship with the Soviet Union in the heels of Stalin's death in 1953.

Prior to re-election, Churchill had already suffered from a mild stroke in 1949. This was followed by another stroke in 1953, which was more severe than the first. Despite this fact, Churchill still showed up for a Cabinet meeting the day after he suffered from the stroke. In the same year, he officially became Sir Winston Churchill after being knighted by the young Queen Elizabeth II. He continued to introduce relevant reforms in the British system such as:

> The Mines and Quarries Act (1954)

> The Housing Repairs and Rent Act (1955)

Churchill suffered a few more minor strokes, though neither the public nor parliament ever found out about it. His body was slowing down and could no longer keep up with the rigors of his job. Finally, he resigned as Prime Minister in 1955 and handed the reigns over to his deputy Anthony Eden. He did not, however, give up his post as a member of parliament and remained so until 1964. He no longer sought re-election in the general elections that year.

Winston Churchill suffered another major stroke on the 15th of January 1965. His body could no longer recover from the strokes. He died on the 24th of January 1965, 70 years to the day of his own father's death. This was also another one of his predictions that eventually came true. For ten years prior to his death, Churchill had been known to tell those who were close to him that he would die on the same day as Lord Randolph. He had shown so much conviction on this belief that in the early morning of January 25, 1965, family and friends had already gathered around his bedside to say their final farewells.

Chapter 9:
The Woman behind the Great Man

So much has been said about Winston Churchill in various editions of history books since the end of WWII. Unfortunately, only a handful of these have focused on the woman whom Churchill himself has credited for his success: his wife, Clementine Hozier Spencer-Churchill. Just like Winston, his wife also had an aristocratic lineage. But this linage is often marred by the continuous questions raised about her paternity. Their lineage is far from the only thing that Winston and Clementine Churchill share.

They both had unhappy childhoods wherein they longed to form closer relationships with their distracted parents. They both possessed keen minds that allowed them to excel in the school subjects that they were most interested in. But unlike Winston, Clementine was not able to get a College degree mostly because her mother never supported her dream of going to university.

When it became apparent to Blanche Hozier that her daughter was in danger of turning into a 'bluestocking', she focused all her efforts in circumventing it. So it was that Clementine embarked on a journey that took her from school to some of the most elegant salons in England. This journey eventually took her to the Lord and Lady Crewe's home in Curzon Street in 1904 where she met the man who would soon change her life: Winston Churchill. She was only nineteen at the time, while Winston was thirty and already past some of his most challenging experiences (including his escape as a POW during the Boer War).

The meeting was brief though Clementine's renowned beauty did make an impression on the young MP. They were introduced to each other by Winston's mother, Lady Randolph Churchill. Nothing special happened on this brief encounter except for the fact that the highly vocal MP was speechless probably for the first (and only) time in his life. Clementine was not impressed by Churchill because she had already heard a lot of unsavory rumors about him.

Churchill did not pursue the attraction, though, because his primary priority was politics. Note that this first meeting happened at around the same time that Churchill was slowly veering away from the Conservative Party to cross the floor over to the Liberals. Their paths didn't cross again until 1908 at a dinner party that neither of them wanted to attend. But they were both compelled to go since the dinner was organized by Lady St Helier, a woman to whom both of them were commonly indebted to due to various favors in the past.

This time, their encounter was no longer as brief as the first one. Throughout the entire dinner party, Winston devoted his attention completely on Clementine and they both left that dinner with good feelings about the other. Things progressed from there until they eventually got married on the 12th of September 1908. To say that they married for love would be an understatement. It was the beginning of a shared life that spanned almost 6 decades and that put Clementine in the public eye for 70 years. They had 5 children together, one of whom died at a young age.

Throughout the course of their marriage, Clementine adeptly navigated the complicated life of her popular (and often unpopular) husband. She not only made many economical changes to his home life, but she also plunged herself fully into the world of politics. Her intelligence and natural zest for life made her the perfect combination for her husband's complex temperament. Early on, Clementine had swayed towards the liberal way of thinking and she stuck to this belief for good. But regardless of her own beliefs, she still displayed her full support to her husband whether he was standing with the Liberals or with the Conservatives.

Their marriage was initially met with disdain by the snobbish members of Britain's elite mostly because Clementine was deemed to be below Winston's station. But she soon proved her worth in her own ways. She advocated for women's education and women's right to vote long before these became an 'in' thing. Her influence on Winston's life was obvious in the fact that people who wanted to sway his mind on some important national issue would often go to Clementine for help. She was known to be the only person who could change her husband's stubborn mind.

Her influence was most felt during WWII. During this time, she often gave Winston her insights on war strategies and would even formulate her own strategies in certain occasions. She also played a leading role on his campaign to woo the US to join the war. She wined and dined some of the leading figures in US politics at their home. On D-day, she also cooperated with King George VI to keep Winston from going through with his foolhardy plan of going out on the HMS Belfast to watch the action up close. She was also a leading figure in many of Winston's election campaigns, often appearing in his stead whenever he was indisposed.

She was also quite protective of her husband and had saved his life a couple of times. One instance of this is when she leapt to his rescue after he was pushed onto the path of a speeding train by a disgruntled suffragette. She may have also saved him from an early death at the height of WWII when he was diagnosed with a deteriorating heart condition. His doctor found that he could suffer from a coronary thrombosis at any time and that the attack could be fatal. The two of them kept this a secret so as not to give him another thing to worry about given the fact that he already carried the fate of the world in his shoulders.

Clementine's contribution to Winston Churchill's life can be summed up in the words of the great man himself: she made his life and all the work that he had done possible.

Clementine passed away on the 12th of December 1977 at the ripe old age of 112.

Chapter 10:
Life Lessons

Despite the fact that Winston Churchill was born into a life of privilege, things never came easy for him. Unlike other children who belonged to his social station, Churchill has repeatedly known failure even from a very young age. He failed to impress his parents, he failed in various exams, he failed in various elections, and so on. But true to his WWI battlecry, Churchill never ever gave up.

He stubbornly plodded on and kept on trying until he finally reached his end-game, be it achieving a high ranking in school or getting elected into the highest post in the government. This stubborn attitude in the face of defeat is something that a lot of people should definitely learn to imitate. Churchill's life is a testament to the fact that your ambitions should never end where your failure begins. That's because failure can best serve as a platform to step on in order to reach higher ground.

Another lesson to learn from the story of such a great man is that age doesn't have to be a hindrance for achieving your greatest dreams. Remember that Churchill was no longer a fresh-faced young MP on his first term as Prime Minister, more so on his second term. Yet he still performed his job to the best that his aging abilities would allow. He refused to allow naysayers to have the final word.

Throughout his political career, Churchill has also had to deal with objections from all sides even when in the end he turned out to be right. But as many of his speeches have proven, once Churchill had set his mind on something, no amount of dissenting opinion could change it. Also note that he came from an aristocratic family, and like many such families in that day, he was often short on cash.

But unlike other nobles who refused to lower themselves down to earn a living, Churchill worked as hard as any commoner to put food on his family's table. He wrote articles, speeches, and books to earn a living. In the end, he was justly rewarded by winning the Nobel Prize in Literature in 1953.

So what is the greatest life lesson that you should take away from the life story of a man who was larger than anyone in his time had ever known? The answer is simple: perseverance is the key towards unlocking all the possibilities. Stand up for something even when the rest of the world is standing against you. Never give up. Never give in.

Conclusion

Thanks again for taking the time to read this book!

You should now have a good understanding of Winston Churchill and his life journey!

If you enjoyed this book, please take the time to leave me a review on Amazon. I appreciate your honest feedback, and it really helps me to continue producing high quality books.